Fifty-two Poems for Men

COMPILED BY DR. JAY AMBERG

AMIKA PRESS

First Edition
ISBN: 0-9708416-0-4
Library of Congress Control Number: 2001090612

Published by Amika Press
2454 Pioneer Street
Evanston, Illinois 60201
(847) 869-8084

Acknowledgements

Thanks to the many people who provided suggestions for poems and who helped in the creation of this book.

I offer special thanks to Elizabeth Haldeman, who designed the book. Without her ingenuity, diligence, and ebullience, *Fifty-two Poems for Men* would not exist.

Table of Contents

Introduction

Men don't like poetry—often with good reason. A lot of poetry is lame, dealing with fuzzy emotional stuff in syrupy fashion. It's enough to give a guy the willies. Other poetry deals with issues that, though certainly a part of life, we'd frankly rather not face—at least until they're inescapable. Either way, we're likely to pass on poetry. Look the other way. Dismiss it outright. Dash for the nearest exit. Even bolt for the country.

A suspicion of poetry is a good thing. Life's too short for fuzz and syrup. The combination's repugnant. But some poems speak to what life's about, what's going on here, what we're all doing. And a few poems do so with stunning clarity. They wap you across the side of the head. Or, cut to the bone, far into the marrow.

I read thousands of poems over the past two years. I talked with people, asking which poems, if any, they liked. I sifted and sorted. Though I didn't have hard and fast rules, I gradually developed guidelines:

- No poems with obscure references, especially to English history
- No poems about poetry
- No clubby poems written for other poets
- No thines and thou arts or other painfully outdated phrases
- No pomposity or gobbledygook
- No translations
- No self-consciously cute forms
- No avant-garde nonsense
- No epigrams, especially in the original Greek or Latin
- No esoteric poems that can't possibly be understood by anyone

And, of course, I ignored each of these guidelines (except the last) at some point when considering particular poems.

I eventually came up with a list of a couple hundred players, poems that might make it into the book. Then I reread and read some more, finally selecting the all-stars—the fifty-two poems that I believed would speak most clearly to you. If any of them snatch your breath, that's the idea. If any shake you awake, that's good. If any cut deep, so much the better.

The themes in these poems aren't new—birth and death, parents and children, growing up, love, loss, war, beauty... all the usual suspects. I did, though, look especially for poems that captured moments, provided glimpses of life, and suggested small insights.

The dimwitted omissions in this book are mine, as are the wrong-headed inclusions. But that's exactly the point. Take from this group whatever grabs you. Reread and reject others. Decide what to hold fast and what to discard. Tear out any poems that offend. Rip them right out of the book. Add your own. But, whatever you do, keep listening to the voices.

Here are fifty-two poems for men. You won't like all of them, but some will speak to you. A few, deeply.

Fifty-two Poems for Men

COMPILED BY DR. JAY AMBERG

AMIKA PRESS

Those Winter Sundays

ROBERT HAYDEN

Sundays too my father got up early
and put his clothes on in the blueblack cold,
then with cracked hands that ached
from labor in the weekday weather made
banked fires blaze. No one ever thanked him.

I'd wake and hear the cold splintering, breaking.
When the rooms were warm, he'd call,
and slowly I would rise and dress,
fearing the chronic angers of that house,

Speaking indifferently to him,
who had driven out the cold
and polished my good shoes as well.
What did I know, what did I know
of love's austere and lonely offices?

Eleven

ARCHIBALD MACLIESH

And summer mornings the mute child, rebellious,
Stupid, hating the words, the meanings, hating
The Think now, Think, the Oh but Think! would leave
On tiptoe the three chairs on the verandah
And crossing tree by tree the empty lawn
Push back the shed door and upon the sill
Stand pressing out the sunlight from his eyes
And enter and with outstretched fingers feel
The grindstone and behind it the bare wall
And turn and in the corner on the cool
Hard earth sit listening. And one by one,
Out of the dazzled shadow in the room,
The shapes would gather, the brown plowshare, spades,
Mattocks, the polished helves of picks, a scythe
Hung from the rafters, shovels, slender tines
Glinting across the curve of sickles—shapes
Older than men were, the wise tools, the iron
Friendly with earth. And sit there quiet, breathing
The harsh dry smell of withered bulbs, the faint
Odor of dung, the silence. And outside
Beyond the half-shut door the blind leaves
And the corn moving. And at noon would come,
Up from the garden, his hard crooked hands
Gentle with earth, his knees still earth-stained, smelling
Of sun, of summer, the old gardener, like
A priest, like an interpreter, and bend
Over his baskets.
            And they would not speak:
They would say nothing. And the child would sit there
Happy as though he had no name, as though
He had been no one: like a leaf, a stem,
Like a root growing—

Mother to Son

LANGSTON HUGHES

Well, son, I'll tell you:
Life for me ain't been no crystal stair.
It's had tacks in it,
And splinters,
And boards torn up,
And places with no carpet on the floor—
Bare.
But all the time
I'se been a-climbin' on,
And reachin' landin's,
And turnin' corners,
And sometimes goin' in the dark
Where there ain't been no light.
So boy, don't you turn back.
Don't you set down on the steps
'Cause you finds it's kinder hard.
Don't you fall now—
For I'se still goin', honey,
I'se still climbin',
And life for me ain't been no crystal stair.

From the Childhood of Jesus

ROBERT PINSKY

One Saturday morning he went to the river to play.
He modeled twelve sparrows out of the river clay

And scooped a clear pond, with a dam of twigs and mud.
Around the pond he set the birds he had made,

Evenly as the hours. Jesus was five. He smiled,
As a child would who had made a little world

Of clear still water and clay beside a river.
But a certain Jew came by, a friend of his father,

And he scolded the child and ran at once to Joseph,
Saying, "Come see how your child has profaned the Sabbath,

Making images at the river on the Day of Rest."
So Joseph came to the place and took his wrist

And told him, "Child, you have offended the Word."
Then Jesus freed the hand that Joseph held

And clapped his hands and shouted to the birds
To go away. They raised their beaks at his words

And breathed and stirred their feathers and flew away.
The people were frightened. Meanwhile, another boy,

The son of Annas the scribe, had idly taken
A branch of driftwood and leaning against it had broken

The dam and muddied the little pond and scattered
The twigs and stones. Then Jesus was angry and shouted,

"Unrighteous, impious, ignorant, what did the water
Do to harm you? Now you are going to wither

The way a tree does, you shall bear no fruit
And no leaves, you shall wither down to the root."

At once, the boy was all withered. His parents moaned,
The Jews gasped, Jesus began to leave, then turned

And prophesied, his child's face wet with tears:
"Twelve times twelve times twelve thousands of years

Before these heavens and this earth were made,
The Creator set a jewel in the throne of God

With Hell on the left and Heaven to the right,
The Sanctuary in front, and behind, an endless night

Endlessly fleeing a Torah written in flame.
And on that jewel in the throne, God wrote my name."

Then Jesus left and went into Joseph's house.
The family of the withered one also left the place,

Carrying him home. The Sabbath was nearly over.
By dusk, the Jews were all gone from the river.

Small creatures came from the undergrowth to drink
And foraged in the shadows along the bank.

Alone in his cot in Joseph's house, the Son
Of Man was crying himself to sleep. The moon

Rose higher, the Jews put out their lights and slept,
And all was calm and as it had been, except

In the agitated household of the scribe Annas,
And high in the dark, where unknown even to Jesus

The twelve new sparrows flew aimlessly through the night,
Not blinking or resting, as if never to alight.

My Papa's Waltz

THEODORE ROETHKE

The whiskey on your breath
Could make a small boy dizzy;
But I hung on like death:
Such waltzing was not easy.

We romped until the pans
Slid from the kitchen shelf;
My mother's countenance
Could not unfrown itself.

The hand that held my wrist
Was battered on one knuckle;
At every step you missed
My right ear scraped a buckle.

You beat time on my head
With a palm caked hard by dirt,
Then waltzed me off to bed
Still clinging to your shirt.

To Look
at
Any Thing

JOHN MOFFITT

To look at any thing,
If you would know that thing,
You must look at it long:
To look at this green and say
'I have seen spring in these
Woods,' will not do—you must
Be the thing you see:
You must be the dark snakes of
Stems and ferny plumes of leaves,
You must enter in
To the small silences between
The leaves,
You must take your time
And touch the very peace
They issue from.

The Box Fan

GARY SOTO

For nine months the box fan held its breath
In the closet. For three months of summer
It rattled the pages
Of *TV Guide*. It was summer now.
My stepfather was drinking Jack Daniels
From a TV tray pressed with the faces
Of our dead and live presidents.
The trouble with you,
He said, is that you don't respect the law.
He had come home from work, fingers black
From book print, the fissures of paper cuts
On the web of skin
Between thumb and index finger.
I had chained my bike to a tree.
He said there were laws against that kind
Of behavior. It hurt the tree. It was an eyesore.
Babies could poke an eye out on the handlebars
And could take away our house.

The sour heat of bourbon cracked the ice.
The pages rattled in the whir of the fan,
Blades the color of spoons and forks falling
From a drawer. I knew
It would take more than a knife to bring him down,
More than a slammed door to jam his heart.
You see my point? he said,
And then asked me to spell implements,
A word he picked up from *TV Guide*.
While I spelled the word,
While I counted out the letters
On my fingers, he drained his bourbon,
The sliver of ice riding the thick chute of throat.
He poured himself another and said,

I like that. I-m-p-l-e-m-e-n-t-s.
It's a good word to know.
He fixed the fan so that my hair stirred
And the pages of the magazine ruffled
From Sunday to Friday. I saw a serious face,
Then a laughing face in those pages,
Ads for steam cleaning and miracle products,
And the shuffle of my favorite nighttime shows.
He said that the trouble with me,
With a lot of young people, is that we can't spell.
He poured an inch of bourbon, with no ice,
And said, Try it again, without your fingers—
I imagined the fan blades and blood jumping to the wall.

We Real Cool

GWENDOLYN BROOKS

THE POOL PLAYERS.
SEVEN AT THE GOLDEN SHOVEL.

We real cool. We
Left school. We

Lurk late. We
Strike straight. We

Sing sin. We
Thin gin. We

Jazz June. We
Die soon.

August from My Desk

ROLAND FLINT

It is hot today, dry enough for cutting grain,
and I am drifting back to North Dakota
where butterflies are all gone brown with wheat dust.

And where some boy,
red-faced, sweating, chafed,
too young to be dying this way
steers a laborious, self-propelled combine,
and dreams of cities, and blizzards—
and airplanes.

With the white silk scarf of his sleeve
he shines and shines his goggles,
he checks his meters, checks his flaps,
screams contact at his dreamless father,
and, engines roaring,
he pulls back the stick

and hurtles into the sun.

A Blessing

JAMES WRIGHT

Just off the highway to Rochester, Minnesota,
Twilight bounds softly forth on the grass.
And the eyes of those two Indian ponies
Darken with kindness.
They have come gladly out of the willows
To welcome my friend and me.
We step over the barbed wire into the pasture
Where they have been grazing all day, alone.
They ripple tensely, they can hardly contain their happiness
That we have come.
They bow shyly as wet swans. They love each other.
There is no loneliness like theirs.
At home once more,
They begin munching the young tufts of spring in the darkness.
I would like to hold the slenderer one in my arms,
For she has walked over to me
And nuzzled my left hand.
She is black and white,
Her mane falls wild on her forehead,
And the light breeze moves me to caress her long ear
That is delicate as the skin over a girl's wrist.
Suddenly I realize
That if I stepped out of my body I would break
Into blossom.

maggie and milly and molly and may

E.E. CUMMINGS

maggie and milly and molly and may
went down to the beach(to play one day)

and maggie discovered a shell that sang
so sweetly she couldn't remember her troubles,and

milly befriended a stranded star
whose rays five languid fingers were;

and molly was chased by a horrible thing
which raced sideways while blowing bubbles:and

may came home with a smooth round stone
as small as a world as large as alone.

For whatever we lose(like a you or a me)
it's always ourselves we find in the sea

The Celebration

JAMES DICKEY

All wheels; a man breathed fire,
Exhaling like a blowtorch down the road
And burnt the stripper's gown
Above her moving-barely feet.
A condemned train climbed from the earth
Up stilted nightlights zooming in a track.
I ambled along in that crowd

Between the gambling wheels
At carnival time with the others
Where the dodgem cars shuddered, sparking
On grillwire, each in his vehicle half
In control, half helplessly power-mad
As he was in the traffic that brought him.
No one blazed at me; then I saw

My mother and my father, he leaning
On a dog-chewed cane, she wrapped to the nose
In the fur of exhausted weasels.
I believed them buried miles back
In the country, in the faint sleep
Of the old, and had not thought to be
On this of all nights compelled

To follow where they led, not losing
Sight, with my heart enlarging whenever
I saw his crippled Stetson bob, saw her
With the teddy bear won on the waning
Whip of his right arm. They laughed;
She clung to him; then suddenly
The Wheel of wheels was turning

The colored night around.
They climbed aboard. My God, they rose
Above me, stopped themselves and swayed

Fifty feet up; he pointed
With his toothed cane, and took in
The whole Midway till they dropped,
Came down, went from me, came and went

Faster and faster, going up backward,
Cresting, out-topping, falling roundly.
From the crowd I watched them,
Their gold teeth flashing,
Until my eyes blurred with their riding
Lights, and I turned from the standing
To the moving mob, and went on:

Stepped upon sparking shocks
Of recognition when I saw my feet
Among the others, knowing them given,
Understanding the whirling impulse
From which I had been born,
The great gift of shaken lights,
The being wholly lifted with another,

All this having all and nothing
To do with me. Believers, I have seen
The wheel in the middle of the air
Where old age rises and laughs,
And on Lakewood Midway became
In five strides a kind of loving,
A mortal, a dutiful son.

To an Athlete Dying Young

A.E. HOUSMAN

The time you won your town the race
We chaired you through the market-place;
Man and boy stood cheering by,
And home we brought you shoulder-high.

To-day, the road all runners come,
Shoulder-high we bring you home,
And set you at your threshold down,
Townsman of a stiller town.

Smart lad, to slip betimes away
From fields where glory does not stay
And early though the laurel grows
It withers quicker than the rose.

Eyes the shady night has shut
Cannot see the record cut,
And silence sounds no worse than cheers
After earth has stopped the ears:

Now you will not swell the rout
Of lads that wore their honours out,
Runners whom renown outran
And the name died before the man.

So set, before its echoes fade,
The fleet foot on the sill of shade,
And hold to the low lintel up
The still-defended challenge-cup.

And round that early-laurelled head
Will flock to gaze the strengthless dead
And find unwithered on its curls
The garland briefer than a girl's.

Naming of Parts

HENRY REED

Today we have naming of parts. Yesterday,
We had daily cleaning. And tomorrow morning,
We shall have what to do after firing. But today,
Today we have naming of parts. Japonica
Glistens like coral in all of the neighboring gardens,
    And today we have naming of parts.

This is the lower sling swivel. And this
Is the upper sling swivel, whose use you will see,
When you are given your slings. And this is the piling swivel,
Which in your case you have not got. The branches
Hold in the gardens their silent, eloquent gestures,
    Which in our case we have not got.

This is the safety-catch, which is always released
With an easy flick of the thumb. And please do not let me
See anyone using his finger. You can do it quite easy
If you have any strength in your thumb. The blossoms
Are fragile and motionless, never letting anyone see
    Any of them using their finger.

And this you can see is the bolt. The purpose of this
Is to open the breech, as you see. We can slide it
Rapidly backwards and forwards: we call this
Easing the spring. And rapidly backwards and forwards
The early bees are assaulting and fumbling the flowers:
    They call it easing the Spring.

They call it easing the Spring: it is perfectly easy
If you have any strength in your thumb: like the bolt
And the breech, and the cocking-piece, and the point of balance,
Which in our case we have not got; and the almond-blossom
Silent in all of the gardens and the bees going backwards and
    forwards,
    For today we have naming of parts.

Dulce et Decorum Est

WILFRED OWEN

Bent double, like old beggars under sacks,
Knock-kneed, coughing like hags, we cursed through sludge,
Till on the haunting flares we turned our backs,
And towards our distant rest began to trudge.
Men marched asleep. Many had lost their boots
But limped on, blood-shod. All went lame; all blind;
Drunk with fatigue; deaf even to the hoots
Of gas-shells dropping softly behind.

Gas! GAS! Quick, boys—An ecstasy of fumbling,
Fitting the clumsy helmets just in time,
But someone still was yelling out and stumbling
And floundering like a man in fire or lime.—
Dim, through the misty panes and thick green light
As under a green sea, I saw him drowning.

In all my dreams before my helpless sight,
He plunges at me, guttering, choking, drowning.

If in some smothering dreams, you too could pace
Behind the wagon that we flung him in,
And watch the white eyes writhing in his face,
His hanging face, like a devil's sick of sin;
If you could hear, at every jolt, the blood
Come gargling from the froth-corrupted lungs,
Obscene as cancer, bitter as the cud
Of vile, incurable sores on innocent tongues,—
My friend, you would not tell with such high zest
To children ardent for some desperate glory,
The old Lie: *Dulce et decorum est*
Pro patria mori.

When I Heard the Learn'd Astronomer

WALT WHITMAN

When I heard the learn'd astronomer,
When the proofs, the figures, were ranged in columns before
    me,
When I was shown the charts and diagrams, to add, divide,
    and measure them,
When I sitting heard the astronomer where he lectured with
    much applause in the lecture-room,
How soon unaccountable I became tired and sick,
Till rising and gliding out I wander'd off by myself,
In the mystical moist night-air, and from time to time,
Look'd up in perfect silence at the stars.

The Road Not Taken

ROBERT FROST

Two roads diverged in a yellow wood,
And sorry I could not travel both
And be one traveler, long I stood
And looked down one as far as I could
To where it bent in the undergrowth;

Then took the other, as just as fair,
And having perhaps the better claim,
Because it was grassy and wanted wear;
Though as for that, the passing there
Had worn them really about the same,

And both that morning equally lay
In leaves no step had trodden black.
Oh, I kept the first for another day!
Yet knowing how way leads on to way,
I doubted if I should ever come back.

I shall be telling this with a sigh
Somewhere ages and ages hence:
Two roads diverged in a wood, and I —
I took the one less traveled by,
And that has made all the difference.

The Men That Don't Fit In

ROBERT SERVICE

There's a race of men that don't fit in,
  A race that can't stay still;
So they break the hearts of kith and kin,
  And they roam the world at will.
They range the field and they rove the flood,
  And they climb the mountain's crest;
Theirs is the curse of the gypsy blood,
  And they don't know how to rest.

If they just went straight they might go far;
  They are strong and brave and true;
But they're always tired of the things that are,
  And they want the strange and new.
They say: "Could I find my proper groove,
  What a deep mark I would make!"
So they chop and change, and each fresh move
  Is only a fresh mistake.

And each forgets, as he strips and runs
  With a brilliant, fitful pace,
It's the steady, quiet, plodding ones
  Who win in the lifelong race.
And each forgets that his youth has fled,
  Forgets that his prime is past,
Till he stands one day, with a hope that's dead,
  In the glare of the truth at last.

He has failed, he has failed; he has missed his chance;
  He has just done things by half.
Life's been a jolly good joke on him,
  And now is the time to laugh.
Ha, ha! He is one of the Legion Lost;
  He was never meant to win;
He's a rolling stone, and it's bred in the bone;
  He's a man who won't fit in.

Pied Beauty

GERARD MANLEY HOPKINS

Glory be to God for dappled things—
   For skies of couple-colour as a brinded cow;
     For rose-moles all in stipple upon trout that swim;
Fresh-firecoal chestnut-falls; finches' wings;
   Landscape plotted and pieced—fold, fallow, and plough;
     And áll trádes, their gear and tackle and trim.

All things counter, original, spare, strange;
   Whatever is fickle, freckled (who knows how?)
     With swift, slow; sweet, sour; adazzle, dim;
He fathers-forth whose beauty is past change:
       Praise him.

Driving Montana

RICHARD HUGO

The day is a woman who loves you. Open.
Deer drink close to the road and magpies
spray from your car. Miles from any town
your radio comes in strong, unlikely
Mozart from Belgrade, rock and roll
from Butte. Whatever the next number,
you want to hear it. Never has your Buick
found this forward a gear. Even
the tuna salad in Reedpoint is good.

Towns arrive ahead of imagined schedule.
Absorakee at one. Or arrive so late—
Silesia at nine—you recreate the day.
Where did you stop along the road
and have fun? Was there a runaway horse?
Did you park at that house, the one
alone in a void of grain, white with green
trim and red fence, where you know you lived
once? You remembered the ringing creek,
the soft brown forms of far off bison.
You must have stayed hours, then drove on.
In the motel you know you'd never seen it before.

Tomorrow will open again, the sky wide
as the mouth of a wild girl, friable
clouds you lose yourself to. You are lost
in miles of land without people, without
one fear of being found, in the dash
of rabbits, soar of antelope, swirl
merge and clatter of streams.

Harlem

LANGSTON HUGHES

What happens to a dream deferred?

Does it dry up
like a raisin in the sun?
Or fester like a sore—
And then run?
Does it stink like rotten meat?
Or crust and sugar over—
like a syrupy sweet?

Maybe it just sags
like a heavy load.

Or does it explode?

Meditation at Lagunitas

ROBERT HASS

All the new thinking is about loss.
In this it resembles all the old thinking.
The idea, for example, that each particular erases
the luminous clarity of a general idea. That the clown-
faced woodpecker probing the dead sculpted trunk
of that black birch is, by his presence,
some tragic falling off from a first world
of undivided light. Or the other notion that,
because there is in this world no one thing
to which the bramble of *blackberry* corresponds,
a word is elegy to what it signifies.
We talked about it late last night and in the voice
of my friend, there was a thin wire of grief, a tone
almost querulous. After a while I understood that,
talking this way, everything dissolves: *justice,
pine, hair, woman, you* and *I*. There was a woman
I made love to and I remembered how, holding
her small shoulders in my hands sometimes,
I felt a violent wonder at her presence
like a thirst for salt, for my childhood river
with its island willows, silly music from the pleasure boat,
muddy places where we caught the little orange-silver fish
called *pumpkinseed*. It hardly had to do with her.
Longing, we say, because desire is full
of endless distances. I must have been the same to her.
But I remember so much, the way her hands dismantled bread,
the thing her father said that hurt her, what
she dreamed. There are moments when the body is as numinous
as words, days that are the good flesh continuing.
Such tenderness, those afternoons and evenings,
saying *blackberry, blackberry, blackberry*.

Musée des Beaux Arts

W. H. AUDEN

About suffering they were never wrong,
The Old Masters: how well they understood
Its human position; how it takes place
While someone else is eating or opening a window or just
   walking dully along;
How, when the aged are reverently, passionately waiting
For the miraculous birth, there always must be
Children who did not specially want it to happen, skating
On a pond at the edge of the wood:
They never forgot
That even the dreadful martyrdom must run its course
Anyhow in a corner, some untidy spot
Where the dogs go on with their doggy life and the torturer's
   horse
Scratches its innocent behind on a tree.

In Breughel's *Icarus*, for instance: how everything turns away
Quite leisurely from the disaster; the ploughman may
Have heard the splash, the forsaken cry,
But for him it was not an important failure; the sun shone
As it had to on the white legs disappearing into the green
Water; and the expensive delicate ship that must have seen
Something amazing, a boy falling out of the sky,
Had somewhere to get to and sailed calmly on.

The Explosion

PHILIP LARKIN

On the day of the explosion
Shadows pointed toward the pithead:
In the sun the slagheap slept.

Down the lane came men in pitboots
Coughing oath-edged talk and pipe-smoke,
Shouldering off the freshened silence.

One chased after rabbits; lost them;
Came back with a nest of lark's eggs;
Showed them; lodged them in the grasses.

So they passed in beards and moleskins,
Fathers, brothers, nicknames, laughter,
Through the tall gates standing open.

At noon, there came a tremor; cows
Stopped chewing for a second; sun,
Scarfed as in a heat-haze, dimmed.

The dead go on before us, they
Are sitting in God's house in comfort,
We shall see them face to face –

Plain as lettering in the chapels
It was said, and for a second
Wives saw men of the explosion

Larger than in life they managed –
Gold as on a coin, or walking
Somehow from the sun towards them,

One showing the eggs unbroken.

The Second Coming

WILLIAM BUTLER YEATS

Turning and turning in the widening gyre
The falcon cannot hear the falconer;
Things fall apart; the centre cannot hold;
Mere anarchy is loosed upon the world,
The blood-dimmed tide is loosed, and everywhere
The ceremony of innocence is drowned;
The best lack all conviction, while the worst
Are full of passionate intensity.

Surely some revelation is at hand;
Surely the Second Coming is at hand.
The Second Coming! Hardly are those words out
When a vast image out of *Spiritus Mundi*
Troubles my sight: somewhere in sands of the desert
A shape with lion body and the head of a man,
A gaze blank and pitiless as the sun,
Is moving its slow thighs, while all about it
Reel shadows of the indignant desert birds.
The darkness drops again; but now I know
That twenty centuries of stony sleep
Were vexed to nightmare by a rocking cradle,
And what rough beast, its hour come round at last,
Slouches towards Bethlehem to be born?

My Heart Leaps Up

WILLIAM WORDSWORTH

My heart leaps up when I behold
  A rainbow in the sky:
So was it when my life began;
So is it now I am a man;
So be it when I shall grow old.
  Or let me die!
The Child is father of the Man;
And I could wish my days to be
Bound each to each by natural piety.

Arizona Midnight

ROBERT PENN WARREN

The grief of the coyote seems to make
Stars quiver whiter over the blankness which
Is Arizona at midnight. In sleeping-bag,
Protected by the looped rampart of anti-rattler horsehair rope,
I take a careful twist, grinding sand on sand,
To lie on my back. I stare. Stars quiver, twitch,
In their infinite indigo. I know
Nothing to tell the stars, who go,
Age on age, along tracks they understand, and
The only answer I have for the coyote would be
My own grief, for which I have no
Tongue — indeed, scarcely understand.
Eastward, I see
No indication of dawn, not yet ready for the scream
Of inflamed distance,
Which is the significance of day.
But dimly I do see
Against that darkness, lifting in blunt agony,
The single great cactus. Once more I hear the coyote
Wail. I strain to make out the cactus. It has
Its own necessary beauty.

Love Calls Us to the Things of This World

RICHARD WILBUR

The eyes open to a cry of pulleys,
And spirited from sleep, the astounded soul
Hangs for a moment bodiless and simple
As false dawn.
                  Outside the open window
The morning air is all awash with angels.

  Some are in bed-sheets, some are in blouses,
Some are in smocks: but truly there they are.
Now they are rising together in calm swells
Of halcyon feeling, filling whatever they wear
With the deep joy of their impersonal breathing;

  Now they are flying in place, conveying
The terrible speed of their omnipresence, moving
And staying like white water; and now of a sudden
They swoon down into so rapt a quiet
That nobody seems to be there.
                      The soul shrinks

  From all that it is about to remember,
From the punctual rape of every blessèd day,
And cries,
          "Oh, let there be nothing on earth but laundry,
Nothing but rosy hands in the rising steam
And clear dances done in the sight of heaven."

  Yet, as the sun acknowledges
With a warm look the world's hunks and colors,
The soul descends once more in bitter love
To accept the waking body, saying now
In a changed voice as the man yawns and rises,

"Bring them down from their ruddy gallows;
Let there be clean linen for the backs of thieves;
Let lovers go fresh and sweet to be undone,
And the heaviest nuns walk in a pure floating
Of dark habits,
                keeping their difficult balance."

Down, Wanton, Down!

ROBERT GRAVES

Down, wanton, down! Have you no shame
That at the whisper of Love's name,
Or Beauty's, presto! up you raise
Your angry head and stand at gaze?

Poor bombard-captain, sworn to reach
The ravelin and effect a breach—
Indifferent what you storm or why,
So be that in the breach you die!

Love may be blind, but Love at least
Knows what is man and what mere beast;
Or Beauty wayward, but requires
More delicacy from her squires.

Tell me, my witless, whose one boast
Could be your staunchness at the post,
When were you made a man of parts
To think fine and profess the arts?

Will many-gifted Beauty come
Bowing to your bald rule of thumb,
Or Love swear loyalty to your crown?
Be gone, have done! Down, wanton, down!

i like my body when it is with your body

E.E. CUMMINGS

i like my body when it is with your
body. It is so quite new a thing.
Muscles better and nerves more.
i like your body. i like what it does,
i like its hows. i like to feel the spine
of your body and its bones,and the trembling
-firm-smooth ness and which i will
again and again and again
kiss, i like kissing this and that of you,
i like, slowly stroking the,shocking fuzz
of your electric fur,and what-is-it comes
over parting flesh....And eyes big love-crumbs,

and possibly i like the thrill

of under me you so quite new

The Lost Pilot

JAMES TATE

Your face did not rot
like the others—the co-pilot,
for example, I saw him

yesterday. His face is corn-
mush: his wife and daughter,
the poor ignorant people, stare

as if he will compose soon.
He was more wronged than Job.
But your face did not rot

like the others—it grew dark,
and hard like ebony;
the features progressed in their

distinction. If I could cajole
you to come back for an evening,
down from your compulsive

orbiting, I would touch you,
read your face as Dallas,
you hoodlum gunner, now,

with the blistered eyes, reads
his braille editions. I would
touch your face as a disinterested

scholar touches an original page.
However frightening, I would
discover you, and I would not

turn you in; I would not make
you face your wife, or Dallas,
or the co-pilot, Jim. You

could return to your crazy
orbiting, and I would not try
to fully understand what

it means to you. All I know
is this: when I see you,
as I have seen you at least

once every year of my life,
spin across the wilds of the sky
like a tiny, African god,

I feel dead. I feel as if I were
the residue of a stranger's life,
that I should pursue you.

My head cocked toward the sky,
I cannot get off the ground,
and, you, passing over again,

fast, perfect, and unwilling
to tell me that you are doing
well, or that it was mistake

that placed you in that world,
and me in this; or that misfortune
placed these worlds in us.

Birches

ROBERT FROST

When I see birches bend to left and right
Across the lines of straighter darker trees,
I like to think some boy's been swinging them.
But swinging doesn't bend them down to stay
As ice storms do. Often you must have seen them
Loaded with ice a sunny winter morning
After a rain. They click upon themselves
As the breeze rises, and turn many-colored
As the stir cracks and crazes their enamel.
Soon the sun's warmth makes them shed crystal shells
Shattering and avalanching on the snow crust –
Such heaps of broken glass to sweep away
You'd think the inner dome of heaven had fallen.
They are dragged to the withered bracken by the load,
And they seem not to break; though once they are bowed
So low for long, they never right themselves:
You may see their trunks arching in the woods
Years afterwards, trailing their leaves on the ground
Like girls on hands and knees that throw their hair
Before them over their heads to dry in the sun.
But I was going to say when Truth broke in
With all her matter of fact about the ice storm,
I should prefer to have some boy bend them
As he went out and in to fetch the cows –
Some boy too far from town to learn baseball,
Whose only play was what he found himself,
Summer or winter, and could play alone.
One by one he subdued his father's trees
By riding them down over and over again
Until he took the stiffness out of them,
And not one but hung limp, not one was left
For him to conquer. He learned all there was
To learn about not launching out too soon

And so not carrying the tree away
Clear to the ground. He always kept his poise
To the top branches, climbing carefully
With the same pains you use to fill a cup
Up to the brim, and even above the brim.
Then he flung outward, feet first, with a swish,
Kicking his way down through the air to the ground.
So was I once myself a swinger of birches.
And so I dream of going back to be.
It's when I'm weary of considerations,
And life is too much like a pathless wood
Where your face burns and tickles with the cobwebs
Broken across it, and one eye is weeping
From a twig's having lashed across it open.
I'd like to get away from earth awhile
And then come back to it and begin over.
May no fate willfully misunderstand me
And half grant what I wish and snatch me away
Not to return. Earth's the right place for love:
I don't know where it's likely to go better.
I'd like to go by climbing a birch tree,
And climb black branches up a snow-white trunk
Toward heaven, till the tree could bear no more,
But dipped its top and set me down again.
That would be good both going and coming back.
One could do worse than be a swinger of birches.

The Olive Wood Fire

GALWAY KINNELL

When Fergus woke crying at night
I would carry him from his crib
to the rocking chair and sit holding him
before the fire of thousand-year-old olive wood,
which it took a quarter-hour of matches
and kindling to get burning right. Sometimes
—for reasons I never knew and he has forgotten—
even after his bottle the big tears
would keep on rolling down his big cheeks
—the left cheek always more brilliant than the right—
and we would sit, some nights for hours,
rocking in the almost lightless light
eking itself out of the ancient wood,
and hold each other against the darkness,
his close behind and far away in the future,
mine I imagined all around.
One such time, fallen half-asleep myself,
I thought I heard a scream
—a flier crying out in horror
as he dropped fire on he didn't know what or whom,
or else a child thus set aflame—
and sat up alert. The olive wood fire
had burned low. In my arms lay Fergus,
fast asleep, left cheek glowing, God.

Ex–Basketball Player

JOHN UPDIKE

Pearl Avenue runs past the high-school lot,
Bends with the trolley tracks, and stops, cut off
Before it has a chance to go two blocks,
At Colonel McComsky Plaza. Berth's Garage
Is on the corner facing west, and there,
Most days, you'll find Flick Webb, who helps Berth out.

Flick stands tall among the idiot pumps—
Five on a side, the old bubble-head style,
Their rubber elbows hanging loose and low.
One's nostrils are two S's, and his eyes
An E and O. And one is squat, without
A head at all—more of a football type.

Once Flick played for the high-school team, the Wizards.
He was good: in fact, the best. In '46
He bucketed three hundred ninety points,
A county record still. The ball loved Flick.
I saw him rack up thirty-eight or forty
In one home game. His hands were like wild birds.

He never learned a trade, he just sells gas,
Checks oil, and changes flats. Once in a while,
As a gag, he dribbles an inner tube,
But most of us remember anyway.
His hands are fine and nervous on the lug wrench.
It makes no difference to the lug wrench, though.

Off work, he hangs around Mae's Luncheonette.
Grease-gray and kind of coiled, he plays pinball,
Smokes those thin cigars, nurses lemon phosphates.
Flick seldom says a word to Mae, just nods
Beyond her face toward bright applauding tiers
Of Necco Wafers, Nibs, and Juju Beads.

Traveling through the Dark

WILLIAM STAFFORD

Traveling through the dark I found a deer
dead on the edge of the Wilson River road.
It is usually best to roll them into the canyon:
that road is narrow; to swerve might make more dead.

By glow of the tail-light I stumbled back of the car
and stood by the heap, a doe, a recent killing;
she had stiffened already, almost cold.
I dragged her off; she was large in the belly.

My fingers touching her side brought me the reason—
her side was warm; her fawn lay there waiting,
alive, still, never to be born.
Beside that mountain road I hesitated.

The car aimed ahead its lowered parking lights;
under the hood purred the steady engine.
I stood in the glare of the warm exhaust turning red;
around our group I could hear the wilderness listen.

I thought hard for us all—my only swerving—,
then pushed her over the edge into the river.

Love Song: I and Thou

ALAN DUGAN

Nothing is plumb, level, or square:
   the studs are bowed, the joists
are shaky by nature, no piece fits
   any other piece without a gap
or pinch, and bent nails
   dance all over the surfacing
like maggots. By Christ
   I am no carpenter. I built
the roof for myself, the walls
   for myself, the floors
for myself, and got
   hung up in it myself. I
danced with a purple thumb
   at this house-warming, drunk
with my prime whiskey: rage.
   Oh I spat rage's nails
into the frame-up of my work:
   it held. It settled plumb,
level, solid, square and true
   for that great moment. Then
it screamed and went on through,
   skewing as wrong the other way.
God damned it. This is hell,
   but I planned it, I sawed it,
I nailed it, and I
   will live in it until it kills me.
I can nail my left palm
   to the left-hand crosspiece but
I can't do everything myself.
   I need a hand to nail the right,
a help, a love, a you, a wife.

Footnote to Howl

ALLEN GINSBERG

Holy! Holy! Holy! Holy! Holy! Holy! Holy! Holy! Holy! Holy! Holy!
Holy! Holy! Holy! Holy!
The world is holy! The soul is holy! The skin is holy! The nose is
holy! The tongue and cock and hand and asshole holy!
Everything is holy! everybody's holy! everywhere is holy!
everyday is in eternity! Everyman's an angel!
The bum's as holy as the seraphim! the madman is holy as you
my soul are holy!
The typewriter is holy the poem is holy the voice is holy the
hearers are holy the ecstasy is holy!
Holy Peter holy Allen holy Solomon holy Lucien holy Kerouac
holy Huncke holy Burroughs holy Cassady holy the unknown
buggered and suffering beggars holy the hideous human
angels!
Holy my mother in the insane asylum! Holy the cocks of the
grandfathers of Kansas!
Holy the groaning saxophone! Holy the bop apocalypse! Holy
the jazzbands marijuana hipsters peace & junk & drums!
Holy the solitudes of skyscrapers and pavements! Holy the
cafeterias filled with the millions! Holy the mysterious rivers
of tears under the streets!
Holy the lone juggernaut! Holy the vast lamb of the middle
class! Holy the crazy shepherds of rebellion! Who digs Los
Angeles IS Los Angeles!
Holy New York Holy San Francisco Holy Peoria & Seattle Holy
Paris Holy Tangiers Holy Moscow Holy Istanbul!
Holy time in eternity holy eternity in time holy the clocks in
space holy the fourth dimension holy the fifth International
holy the Angel in Moloch!
Holy the sea holy the desert holy the railroad holy the locomotive
holy the visions holy the hallucinations holy the miracles holy
the eyeball holy the abyss!

Holy forgiveness! mercy! charity! faith! Holy! Ours! bodies!
  suffering! magnanimity!
Holy the supernatural extra brilliant intelligent kindness of the soul!

My Mistress' Eyes

WILLIAM SHAKESPEARE

My mistress' eyes are nothing like the sun;
Coral is far more red than her lips red;
If snow be white, why then her breasts are dun;
If hairs be wires, black wires grow on her head.
I have seen roses damask'd, red and white,
But no such roses see I in her cheeks;
And in some perfumes is there more delight
Than in the breath that from my mistress reeks.

I love to hear her speak, yet well I know
That music hath a far more pleasing sound;
I grant I never saw a goddess go;
My mistress, when she walks, treads on the ground:
And yet, by heaven, I think my love as rare
As any she belied with false compare.

This Is Just to Say

WILLIAM CARLOS WILLIAMS

I have eaten
the plums
that were in
the icebox

and which
you were probably
saving
for breakfast

Forgive me
they were delicious
so sweet
and so cold

Men at Forty

DONALD JUSTICE

Men at forty
Learn to close softly
The doors to rooms they will not be
Coming back to.

At rest on a stair landing,
They feel it
Moving beneath them now like the deck of a ship,
Though the swell is gentle.

And deep in mirrors
They rediscover
The face of the boy as he practices tying
His father's tie there in secret

And the face of that father,
Still warm with the mystery of lather.
They are more fathers than sons themselves now.
Something is filling them, something

That is like the twilight sound
Of the crickets, immense,
Filling the woods at the foot of the slope
Behind their mortgaged houses.

Twenty-year Marriage

Ai

You keep me waiting in a truck
with its one good wheel stuck in the ditch,
while you piss against the south side of a tree.
Hurry. I've got nothing on under my skirt tonight.
That still excites you, but this pickup has no windows
and the seat, one fake leather thigh,
pressed close to mine is cold.
I'm the same size, shape, make as twenty years ago,
but get inside me, start the engine;
you'll have the strength, the will to move.
I'll pull, you push, we'll tear each other in half.
Come on, baby, lay me down on my back.
Pretend you don't owe me a thing
and maybe we'll roll out of here,
leaving the past stacked up behind us;
old newspapers nobody's ever got to read again.

Auto Wreck

KARL SHAPIRO

Its quick soft silver bell beating, beating,
And down the dark one ruby flare
Pulsing out red like an artery,
The ambulance at top speed floating down
Past beacons and illuminated clocks
Wings in a heavy curve, dips down,
And brakes speed, entering the crowd.
The doors leap open, emptying light;
Stretchers are laid out, the mangled lifted
And stowed into the little hospital.
Then the bell, breaking the hush, tolls once,
And the ambulance with its terrible cargo
Rocking, slightly rocking, moves away,
As the doors, an afterthought, are closed.

We are deranged, walking among the cops
Who sweep glass and are large and composed.
One is still making notes under the light.
One with a bucket douches ponds of blood
Into the street and gutter.
One hangs lanterns on the wrecks that cling,
Empty husks of locusts, to iron poles.

Our throats were tight as tourniquets,
Our feet were bound with splints, but now,
Like convalescents intimate and gauche,
We speak through sickly smiles and warn
With the stubborn saw of common sense,
The grim joke and the banal resolution.
The traffic moves around with care,
But we remain, touching a wound
That opens to our richest horror.
Already old, the question Who shall die?
Becomes unspoken Who is innocent?

For death in war is done by hands;
Suicide has cause and stillbirth, logic;
And cancer, simple as a flower, blooms.
But this invites the occult mind,
Cancels our physics with a sneer,
And splatters all we knew of denouement
Across the expedient and wicked stones.

I Knew a Woman

THEODORE ROETHKE

I knew a woman, lovely in her bones,
When small birds sighed, she would sigh back at them;
Ah, when she moved, she moved more ways than one:
The shapes a bright container can contain!
Of her choice virtues only gods should speak,
Or English poets who grew up on Greek
(I'd have them sing in chorus, cheek to cheek).

How well her wishes went! She stroked my chin,
She taught me Turn, and Counter-turn, and Stand;
She taught me Touch, that undulant white skin;
I nibbled meekly from her proffered hand;
She was the sickle; I, poor I, the rake,
Coming behind her for her pretty sake
(But what prodigious mowing we did make).

Love likes a gander, and adores a goose:
Her full lips pursed, the errant note to seize;
She played it quick, she played it light and loose;
My eyes, they dazzled at her flowing knees;
Her several parts could keep a pure repose,
Or one hip quiver with a mobile nose
(She moved in circles, and those circles moved).

Let seed be grass, and grass turn into hay:
I'm martyr to a motion not my own;
What's freedom for? To know eternity.
I swear she cast a shadow white as stone.
But who would count eternity in days?
These old bones live to learn her wanton ways:
(I measure time by how a body sways).

Two Hangovers

JAMES WRIGHT

NUMBER ONE

I slouch in bed.
Beyond the streaked trees of my window,
All groves are bare.
Locusts and poplars change to unmarried women
Sorting slate from anthracite
Between railroad ties:
The yellow-bearded winter of the depression
Is still alive somewhere, an old man
Counting his collection of bottle caps
In a tarpaper shack under the cold trees
Of my grave.

I still feel half drunk,
And all those old women beyond my window
Are hunching toward the graveyard.

Drunk, mumbling Hungarian,
The sun staggers in,
And his big stupid face pitches
Into the stove.
For two hours I have been dreaming
Of green butterflies searching for diamonds
In coal seams;
And children chasing each other for a game
Through the hills of fresh graves.
But the sun has come home drunk from the sea,
And a sparrow outside
Sings of the Hanna Coal Co. and the dead moon.
The filaments of cold light bulbs tremble
In music like delicate birds.
Ah, turn it off.

NUMBER TWO: I TRY TO WAKEN AND GREET THE WORLD ONCE AGAIN

In a pine tree,
A few yards away from my window sill,
A brilliant blue jay is springing up and down, up and down,
On a branch.
I laugh, as I see him abandon himself
To entire delight, for he knows as well as I do
That the branch will not break.

Taking Off My Clothes

CAROLYN FORCHE

I take off my shirt, I show you.
I shaved the hair out under my arms.
I roll up my pants, I scraped off the hair
on my legs with a knife, getting white.

My hair is the color of chopped maples
My eyes dark as beans cooked in the south.
(Coal fields in the moon on torn-up hills)

Skin polished as a Ming bowl
showing its blood cracks, its age, I have hundreds
of names for the snow, for this, all of them quiet.

In the night I come to you and it seems a shame.
to waste my deepest shudders on a wall of a man.

You recognize strangers,
think you lived through destruction.
You can't explain this night, my face, your memory.

You want to know what I know?
Your own hands are lying.

Suck It Up

PAUL ZIMMER

Two pugs on the undercard step through
The ropes in satin robes,
Pink Adidas with tassels,
Winking at the women in the crowd.
At instructions they stare down hard
And refuse to touch their gloves,
Trying to make everyone believe
That this will be a serious dust-up.

But when the bell rings they start
Slapping like a couple of Barbie Dolls.
One throws a half-hearted hook,
The other flicks out his jab,
They bounce around for a while
Then grab each other for a tango.
The crowd gets tired of booing
And half of them go out for beer,
But I've got no place to hide.

A week after a cancer scare,
A year from a detached retina,
Asthmatic, overweight, trickling,
Drooling, bent like a blighted elm
In my pajamas and slippers,
I have tuned up my hearing aids to sit in
Numbness without expectation before
These televised Tuesday Night Fights.

With a minute left in the fourth,
Scuffling, they butt their heads
By accident. In midst of all the catcalls
And hubbub suddenly they realize
How much they hate each other.
They start hammering and growling,

Really dealing, whistling combinations,
Hitting on the breaks and thumbing.
At last one guy crosses a stiff jab
With a roundhouse right and the other
Loses his starch. The guy wades into
The wounded one, pounding him
Back and forth until he goes down,
Bouncing his head hard on the canvas.

The count begins but he is saved
By the bell and his trainers haul
Him to his stool as the lens zooms in.

I come to the edge of my La-Z-Boy,
Blinking and groaning from my incision,
Eager for wise, insightful instruction.

He gets a bucket of water in his face,
A sniff on the salts while the cutman
Tries to close his wounds with glue.
His nose is broken, eyes are crossed,
His lips bleed like two rare steaks.
His cornermen take turns slapping his cheeks.
"Suck it up!" they shout.
"Suck it up!"

Variation on the Word *Sleep*

MARGARET ATWOOD

I would like to watch you sleeping,
which may not happen.
I would like to watch you,
sleeping. I would like to sleep
with you, to enter
your sleep as its smooth dark wave
slides over my head

and walk with you through that lucent
wavering forest of bluegreen leaves
with its watery sun & three moons
towards the cave where you must descend,
towards your worst fear

I would like to give you the silver
branch, the small white flower, the one
word that will protect you
from the grief at the center
of your dream, from the grief
at the center. I would like to follow
you up the long stairway
again & become
the boat that would row you back
carefully, a flame
in two cupped hands
to where your body lies
beside me, and you enter
it as easily as breathing in

I would like to be the air
that inhabits you for a moment
only. I would like to be that unnoticed
& that necessary.

So, We'll Go No More A-Roving

GEORGE GORDON, LORD BYRON

So, we'll go no more a-roving
   So late into the night,
Though the heart be still as loving,
   And the moon be still as bright.

For the sword outwears its sheath,
   And the soul wears out the breast,
And the heart must pause to breathe,
   And Love itself have rest.

Though the night was made for loving,
   And the day returns too soon,
Yet we'll go no more a-roving
   By the light of the moon.

Ozymandias

PERCY BYSSHE SHELLEY

I met a traveler from an antique land
Who said: Two vast and trunkless legs of stone
Stand in the desert. Near them, on the sand,
Half sunk, a shattered visage lies, whose frown,
And wrinkled lip, and sneer of cold command,
Tell that its sculptor well those passions read
Which yet survive, stamped on these lifeless things,
The hand that mocked them, and the heart that fed:
And on the pedestal these words appear:
"My name is Ozymandias, king of kings:
Look on my works, ye Mighty, and despair!"
Nothing beside remains. Round the decay
Of that colossal wreck, boundless and bare
The lone and level sands stretch far away.

Happiness Is the Art of Being Broken

BRUCE DAWE

Happiness is the art of being broken
With least sound. The old, whom circumstance
Has ground smooth as green bottle-glass
On the sea's furious grindstone, very often
Practice it to perfection. (For them, death
Is the one definitive shrug
In an infinite series, all prior gestures
Take relevance from this, as much express
Sorrow for stiff canary or cold son.)

Always the first fragmentation
Stirs us to fear...Beyond that point
We learn where we belong, in what uncaring
Complex depths we roll, lashed by light,
Tumbling in anemone-dazzled fathoms
Seek innocence in surrender,
Senility an ironic act of charity
Easing the agony of disparateness until
That day when, all identity lost, we serve
As curios for children roaming beaches,
Makeshift monocles through which they view
The same green transitory world we also knew.

Ulysses

ALFRED, LORD TENNYSON

It little profits that an idle king,
By this still hearth, among these barren crags,
Matched with an aged wife, I mete and dole
Unequal laws unto a savage race,
That hoard, and sleep, and feed, and know not me.
I cannot rest from travel; I will drink
Life to the lees. All times I have enjoyed
Greatly, have suffered greatly, both with those
That loved me, and alone; on shore, and when
Through scudding drifts the rainy Hyades
Vexed the dim sea. I am become a name;
For always roaming with a hungry heart
Much have I seen and known—cities of men
And manners, climates, councils, governments,
Myself not least, but honoured of them all—
And drunk delight of battle with my peers,
Far on the ringing plains of windy Troy.
I am a part of all that I have met;
Yet all experience is an arch wherethrough
Gleams that untraveled world whose margin fades
For ever and for ever when I move.
How dull it is to pause, to make an end,
To rust unburnished, not to shine in use!
As though to breathe were life! Life piled on life
Were all too little, and of one to me
Little remains; but every hour is saved
From that eternal silence, something more,
A bringer of new things; and vile it were
For some three suns to store and hoard myself,
And this gray spirit yearning in desire
To follow knowledge like a sinking star,
Beyond the utmost bound of human thought.

This is my son, mine own Telemachus,
To whom I leave the scepter and the isle—
Well-loved of me, discerning to fulfill
This labor, by slow prudence to make mild
A rugged people, and through soft degrees
Subdue them to the useful and the good.
Most blameless is he, centered in the sphere
Of common duties, decent not to fail
In offices of tenderness, and pay
Meet adoration to my household gods,
When I am gone. He works his work, I mine.

There lies the port; the vessel puffs her sail;
There gloom the dark, broad seas. My mariners,
Souls that have toiled, and wrought, and thought with me—
That ever with a frolic welcome took
The thunder and the sunshine, and opposed
Free hearts, free foreheads—you and I are old;
Old age hath yet his honour and his toil.
Death closes all; but something ere the end,
Some work of noble note, may yet be done,
Not unbecoming men that strove with gods.
The lights begin to twinkle from the rocks;
The long day wanes; the slow moon climbs; the deep
Moans round with many voices. Come, my friends,
'Tis not too late to seek a newer world.
Push off, and sitting well in order smite
The sounding furrows; for my purpose holds
To sail beyond the sunset, and the baths
Of all the western stars, until I die.
It may be that the gulfs will wash us down;
It may be we shall touch the Happy Isles,
And see the great Achilles, whom we knew.

Though much is taken, much abides; and though
We are not now that strength which in old days
Moved earth and heaven, that which we are, we are, –
One equal temper of heroic hearts,
Made weak by time and fate, but strong in will
To strive, to seek, to find, and not to yield.

Do Not Go Gentle into That Good Night

DYLAN THOMAS

Do not go gentle into that good night,
Old age should burn and rave at close of day;
Rage, rage against the dying of the light.

Though wise men at their end know dark is right,
Because their words had forked no lightning they
Do not go gentle into that good night.

Good men, the last wave by, crying how bright
Their frail deeds might have danced in a green bay,
Rage, rage against the dying of the light.

Wild men who caught and sang the sun in flight,
And learn, too late, they grieved it on its way,
Do not go gentle into that good night.

Grave men, near death, who see with blinding sight
Blind eyes could blaze like meteors and be gay,
Rage, rage against the dying of the light.

And you, my father, there on the sad height,
Curse, bless, me now with your fierce tears, I pray.
Do not go gentle into that good night.
Rage, rage against the dying of the light.

Credits

AI "Twenty-Year Marriage". Copyright © 1973 by Ai, from *VICE: New and Selected Poems* by Ai. Used by Permission of W. W. Norton & Company, Inc.

MARGARET ATWOOD "Variation On the Word "Sleep"" from *Selected Poems II: Poems Selected and New 1976-1986* by Margaret Atwood. Copyright © 1987 by Margaret Atwood. Reprinted by permission of Houghton Mifflin Company. All rights reserved.

W. H. AUDEN "Musée des Beaux Arts" from *W. H. Auden Collected Poems* by W. H. Auden. Copyright © 1940 & renewed 1968 by W. H. Auden. Reprinted by permission of Random House, Inc.

GWENDOLYN BROOKS "We Real Cool" by Gwendolyn Brooks. From *Blacks, Third World Press, Chicago.* © 1991 Gwendolyn Brooks. Used by permission of author.

E.E. CUMMINGS "i like my body when it is with your". Copyright 1923, 1925, 1951, 1953, © 1991 by the Trustees for the E.E. Cummings Trust. Copyright © 1976 by George James Firmage, "maggie and milly and molly and may". Copyright © 1956, 1984, 1991 by the Trustees for the E.E. Cummings Trust. Copyright © 1978 by George James Firmage, from *Complete Poems: 1904-1962* by E.E. Cummings, edited by George J. Firmage. Used by permission of Liveright Publishing Corporation.

BRUCE DAWE "Happiness is the Art of Being Broken" from *Condolences of the Season*. Reprinted by permission of Pearson Education Australia.

JAMES DICKEY "The Celebration" from *Poems 1957-1967* © James Dickey. Reprinted by permission of University Press of New England

ALAN DUGAN "Love Song: I and Thou" by Alan Dugan from *New and Collected Poems, 1961-1983*. Reprinted by permission of the author.

ROLAND FLINT "August From My Desk" by Roland Flint © Roland Flint. Used by permission of author

CAROLYN FORSCHE "Taking Off my Clothes" by Carolyn Forsche from *Gathering the Tribes* © 1976 by Carolyn Forsche. Reprinted by permission of Yale University Press.

ROBERT FROST "Birches" and "The Road Not Taken" from *The Poetry of Robert Frost* by Robert Frost edited by Edward Connery Lathem, © 1969 by Henry Holt and Co. Reprinted by permission of Henry Holt & Co., LLC.

ALLEN GINSBERG "Footnote to Howl" from *Collected Poems 1947-1980* by Allen Ginsberg. Copyright © 1955 by Allen Ginsberg. Copyright Renewed. Reprinted by permission of HarperCollins Publishers, Inc.

ROBERT GRAVES "Down, Wanton, Down!" from *Collected Poems* by Robert Graves. Reprinted by permission of Carcanet Press Limited.

About the author

Jay Amberg is a writer and teacher. His six books include the mystery thrillers *Deep Gold* and *Blackbird Singing*. His third mystery novel, *Doubloon*, will be published in March, 2002.

Colophon

Design by Elizabeth Haldeman and Pivot Design, Inc. The layout of the book was composed using Quark XPress. The text was set in Berthold Akzidenz Grotesk from Adobe Systems.